Ikigai/Kintsugi

Avneet K Seehra

BookLeaf
Publishing

Ikigai/Kintsugi © 2022 Avneet K Seehra

All rights reserved.

Presentation by *BookLeaf Publishing*

Web: www.bookleafpub.com

E-mail: info@bookleafpub.com

ISBN: 9789357445306

First edition 2022

DEDICATION

I hope these poems find their way in some shape or form to all those who question their reason for existing.

ACKNOWLEDGEMENT

Thank you to my family for being by my side, watching anime with me and encouraging me to publish my poems.

PREFACE

I always used to think to myself that these tragedies could always be worse. However, that denies one's pain, it's as if I cannot be sad as people are in worse places than me. This isn't the point though. I simply needed to stop comparisons and look at my own pain for what it is and accept it. On the journey to publish these poems I wanted people to feel it's okay to be sad and to focus on their now, not their past. I hope you find some solace in these poems.

Trains

On the train to the past
I look forward and back
A present, a future and a nothing

The blackness swallows the train
Whole as we enter the tunnel
Maybe the longest tunnel I've ever seen
It felt like an eternity stumbling in the darkness

I wait to hear your voice
All that resounds is the sound of silence
I realise on this train
I'm alone

I wish too many things that would never happen
A train to the past leads nowhere
And regrets are felt all around
As you give up again and again and again

The cold seeps into ones bones
Freezing them as hope is all that is left
But even that leaves
There's no reason to go to the future
But now there's even more reason to not go back

You laugh and dance in the embrace of the
darkness

Let's stay in the present.

Falling Desperately into Yourself and the World

If I lose it all now,
Can I regain what I lost?

Looking for the shrouds of misery around me,
I jump leaving it all behind,
I fall.

Can I blind myself to it all?
What did I lose?
It no longer matters
Who I was and
Who I am are gone now
-forever.

Hollow, hopeless and empty,
What was it?
Everything seems to be
Complete
But I know it has been left
Unfinished.

I jump leaving it all behind,
I fall and…

Crimson dyes the ground.
Too late.
I am dead.

Maybe we will meet again
In our next lives.

The red string that binds us
Will not be cut.…
Or has it already been?

Of Stars and Earth and Water Filled Oceans

I searched for the stars
and
Crashed to Earth.
Though the way
I flew was untrodden
with the scent of the wind and the steps of the
stars…
forgotten - erased.
However, you cannot walk on air.
That was a mistake to think so and try.
I had no wings,
nor feathers,
nor powers
Yet I still dared. "Ironic, isn't it?"
I searched from above to down below where
the world was a globe I could hold in my hands.
It shook and in place of snow
red and colourless things covered it.
I know a path through this to reach above.
Try I did, but mistakes were made.
When I crashed to Earth
I realised what a waste it had been.
To kill myself faster to float

Even as I wanted to drown.
So, no I didn't crash to Earth
I drowned in the sea long ago.

Save My Song

"Save me a song of all things miraculous" she
had said.

Those words etched deeply into my heart
I am unable to forget.
The melodic way words fell out of her mouth
and captivated me.

I watched her and
those words she uttered scared me.

She and I were existing peacefully
Even so we were split.

The inner and outer truth shows two sides
unbeknownst to many.

Those last days we talked,
reconciled.

But being with her made
my nature masochistic
and
my heart melancholy.

Used to slicing my heart
and
putting it back together.
Again.

I left…left her.

Finding
We could never meet again.
Striving
to fulfil her last wish.

Only connected in spirit and memories.

Save Me a Lifeboat

Gazing at the blue ocean
we walked
Our backs turned away.

We could no longer
call out.
Our voices
stolen.

We tried to persist
against the current
But pulling us in,
it drowned us

No longer afloat or swimming
We desperately try to keep our head above
water.

The current increases
and
our outstretched arms hold each other
It is ceaseless and
we are pulled apart

Drowning we search for each other

to keep afloat

Neither found
 and our backs are turned away.

Walk on the seabed with only a lantern
to guide.
Wander around like prey
Or corpses.

Our noble selves
and ideals
Watching as they fell off
one by one.

The same as normal.

Our new selves dragging our feet on the seabed
with our backs turned.
We passed the point of no return long ago.

Rainbows

A silver lining in a cloud
That rains rainbows down
Can you see it?

The windows obscure it.

Outside dripping wet
You gaze at the sky
Why is it so beautiful?

The way it kisses the ground and deprives it
elsewhere.

If I was a cloud I would fall to Earth
Like a lover long parted
And once again whole.

However, we always must split.

I love you.
Yet love is not enough
Even fate defying love.

We cannot be together.
Please kill me now
Or let us separate forever.

Wound

I lean over to pick up the broken shards,
But prick myself.

Blood pours out the wound,
It does not stop.

I look for a bandage,
To no avail,
There are only rags and shards.

The white is being painted deep red,
With little white left the wound heals.

I go back to picking up shards,
But more gently with care and kindness,
It does not prick me.

Finally, all the pieces are fitted together,
Some white,
Others red.

It leaves the image of a heart - Shattered but
whole again.

Monsters

This world is a cracked mirror,
And
We are cracked mirrors.

But we are only part of one,
The pieces are all there,
Yet it is still cracked.

Maybe,
before the mirror was not cracked?
Does this mean
the mirror
could lose pieces?

Imagine that,
A world without…

People hide among each other,
No one notices.

We can all be called monsters
….and we can all be called good.

Neither are wrong,
Neither are true.
People are two.
We are not one.

To Trust with Unseen Eyes to Spy

They told her nothing was worth
giving her life for
But she found something which was.
It defied them and they grew angry.
She still persisted.

She travelled and taught
-taught people how to live.
This secret art was forbidden
And they pulled her back.
A monster she was called.

She had only taught them
what she learnt from them.
Was it such a sin - ironic though,
She knew now she had to change.
The thing she was able to give her life for no
longer existed.

She is alone now.
She wanted them to support her and she to
protect them.

However, for her truth and ideals too grand
A martyr she was made - or a living corpse?
Only one subtle difference.

Two Reasons

Who was the one who decided to live this life?
It was you, wasn't it?

Stop talking to me.
You're the one who decided to mock me.

Why can't you feel the light of day?
Did you lose 'that' too?

It happened because I decided to live this life.
Everything - even 'that' - is lost for me.

Why don't you run far, far away?
Leave here because you know you can't stay?

How can I run from fate - I tried, but…No.
I can't stay - I want to leave, yet…

We, me - no, I deign this the only way.
I lost 'that' - emotions, no longer do I
understand.

No longer can I stay.
'An empty human shell'.

For a Small Firefly

Our lives are like fireflies
And we ourselves too.

One moment a bright chartreuse,
The next disillusioned and dark.

The contradiction in our lives
and ourselves,
Two halves
and one whole.
It's amusement to be denied
and baffled with,
Though we are ignorant.

Bright fireflies provide light to all
and burn out,
Dimly lit ones fade
and turn invisible
to become a part of the landscape.
The others only continue along restlessly.

A unprovided glance upon both sides,
No labels or categories,
-they just are.
The existence of these fireflies.

Looking

Dark clouds cover the sky.
It will thunder soon.
I am still looking for you.

So what?

Like stars
Falling from the
Sky
You were
Beautiful
As you gave up
And gave in.

The starlight tresses
Of the milky way illuminating your
Tears.
The deep reds of blood
And iron and love and hate
Dripping from your skin
As you sighed.

It was the end.
There is no point.

You suddenly recalled some words from
Before:
If you cannot save it at the end, then
Just leave it.

You had said that to them a while ago.
Goodbye.

Why?

And in the ends of the thread
that came undone unique
was nothing.
Simply an unravelling of another person.

The threads woven and caught in
irregular, messy ways - chaotic
yet reminders of magic.
Order in chaos and
chaos in order.
Hard to decipher and even harder to live with.

Love uncommon for different and somehow
We live in a world where
individuality is lost, suppressed and
Where only agendas live on.

In the end the threads will unravel
as nothing is left.
The marks of ones' existence lost.

I hope to live in the now where proof of my
existence
Will be recorded once, fully
before ashes to ashes…
You know the rest.

Breathing in Starlight

There was starlight in her hair
And it tortured me.
The way it shone so beautifully
To reveal her universe.

But life and intentions are subjective,
She only saw dust here.
Chartreuse, crimson, azure, magenta
Colours of her world or was it monochrome?

A melancholia enveloped my view
And seeing hers I hoped to remove it.
Like a sickness in the soul I would fall.
Being damned was worth saving her.

The starlight in her hair tortures me still
However, she's alive now.
Her simple answer was found
And mine lost somehow.

Requited

If this could be true
then let me meet
you in the space between,
Where I am me and
you are only you.
The obligations, responsibilities, burdens,
politics
all cast aside once
for a genuine meeting.
Friend or foe irrelevant and
I love yous simple and constant,
unaffected by the wilting of flowers.
These memories pressed in a book,
words and patterns reflections of our time.

Amuse Me, Muses

Three lives
Three worlds
Who knows?

Perhaps more
Or less
This pursuit of knowledge

The past long forgotten
In dusty books
As it retraces and remakes the future

Full of intrigue and lost wonder
It promised you and me something else
That still eludes us

Blood and flesh and bone and dirt
All we can see.

I ask you
What is the answer

No reply yet.

Autumn's Youth

The breath of the earth
And the feel of soil beneath one's feet
A forgotten home.
It is irrelevant.

The cacophony of the sounds of the world
Their intermingling and links...
We talk of the same
Yet it is unrecognisable.

A lost language and medium.
We are hidden in our microcosms
And play using our persona,
whilst hiding shadows.

The end and beginning are in sight in the
middle.
A living present,
Though we are lost to the reminder.
No one cares.
The autumn of youth.

Broken Hopes &
Dreams Part 1

I believed in that
Spring you
Would meet me
And that
I would meet
you.

That seems impossible now.
The flowers
are blooming beautifully
here?

How about
where you are?
I suppose they
Must be starting to bud.

This is why
I planted
Forget-me-nots.

I hope you realise.

Broken Hopes &
Dreams Part 2

In the spring
You never returned.

I waited and waited.
Always gazing at the
flowers you planted.

The peach blossom tree
didn't bloom this year.
Left barren and unappreciated.
Its' branches laden with the
Weight of wishes tied to it.

I wonder whose name…no
Are you still thinking of me

Gentle Breeze

The gentle breeze outside
It ruffled the leaves perturbing them.
I who was looking at them found it beautiful.
These small moments now meant so much more than
Any birthdays or parties or everyday monotony.

Remembering the past never came easily
But these moments I close my eyes to a
Hopeful reminisce.
Wondering about freedom
And chains
That pull me into the past
Backwards.

The melancholic day observed itself
And turned over to night
Waiting for the morning of lovers to reach.
But it was too late.
Everything has already passed.

Drowned and burdened by the
Weight
Of memories.
I continue to live empty.

I wanted to live
But death was sweeter.

I wanted to die
But life was still precious.

The gentle breeze runs off with my hat.
Maybe it is leading me somewhere again.

www.ingramcontent.com/pod-product-compliance
Lightning Source LLC
Chambersburg PA
CBHW070723160726
48003CB00006BA/2357